50 Desserts without an Oven

By: Kelly Johnson

Table of Contents

- No-Bake Cheesecake
- Chocolate Mousse
- Panna Cotta
- Rice Pudding
- Fruit Salad
- Tiramisu
- Chocolate Covered Strawberries
- Coconut Ladoo
- Key Lime Pie (No-Bake)
- Parfaits
- Strawberry Shortcake (No-Bake)
- Ice Cream Sundae
- Cookie Dough Truffles
- Chia Seed Pudding
- Pudding Cups
- Energy Bites
- Mocha Chocolate Truffles
- Fruit Tart (No-Bake)
- Banana Pudding
- Lemon Bars (No-Bake)
- S'mores Dip
- Chocolate Bark
- Peanut Butter Balls
- No-Bake Oatmeal Cookies
- Marshmallow Fluff Dip
- Avocado Chocolate Mousse
- Frozen Yogurt Bark
- Gelato
- Frozen Banana Bites
- Meringue Cookies
- Smoothie Bowl
- Frozen Cheesecake Bites
- Sweet Potato Pie (No-Bake)
- Nutella Mousse
- Agar Jelly
- Sweetened Condensed Milk Pudding

- Fruit and Yogurt Cups
- Rice Crispy Treats
- No-Bake Granola Bars
- Chocolate Avocado Pudding
- Orange Panna Cotta
- Lemon Coconut Energy Bites
- No-Bake Pumpkin Pie
- Berry Crumble (Stovetop)
- Chocolate Chip Cookie Ice Cream Sandwiches
- Peanut Butter Fudge
- Tofu Chocolate Pudding
- Raw Vegan Brownies
- Chocolate Coconut Truffles
- Fruit Popsicles

No-Bake Cheesecake

Ingredients:

- 1 ½ cups graham cracker crumbs
- ½ cup unsalted butter (melted)
- 2 cups cream cheese (softened)
- 1 cup powdered sugar
- 1 teaspoon vanilla extract
- 1 cup heavy whipping cream (whipped)

Instructions:

1. **Prepare crust**: Mix graham cracker crumbs with melted butter and press into the bottom of a springform pan.
2. **Make filling**: In a bowl, beat cream cheese until smooth. Gradually add powdered sugar and vanilla, mixing until well combined.
3. **Fold in cream**: Gently fold in the whipped cream until smooth.
4. **Chill**: Pour the filling into the crust and refrigerate for at least 4 hours or until set.

Chocolate Mousse

Ingredients:

- 1 cup dark chocolate (chopped)
- 3 tablespoons butter
- 3 large eggs (separated)
- ¼ cup sugar
- 1 cup heavy cream (whipped)

Instructions:

1. **Melt chocolate**: In a bowl, melt chocolate and butter together over a double boiler.
2. **Beat egg yolks**: In another bowl, beat egg yolks with sugar until thick.
3. **Combine**: Stir melted chocolate into the yolk mixture.
4. **Fold in egg whites**: In a separate bowl, whip egg whites until stiff peaks form and fold into the chocolate mixture.
5. **Add cream**: Gently fold in whipped cream.
6. **Chill**: Spoon into serving dishes and refrigerate until set.

Panna Cotta

Ingredients:

- 2 cups heavy cream
- ½ cup sugar
- 1 teaspoon vanilla extract
- 2 teaspoons gelatin (powdered)
- 3 tablespoons cold water

Instructions:

1. **Bloom gelatin**: Sprinkle gelatin over cold water and let sit for 5 minutes.
2. **Heat cream**: In a saucepan, heat heavy cream, sugar, and vanilla until sugar dissolves.
3. **Combine**: Remove from heat, add bloomed gelatin, and stir until dissolved.
4. **Chill**: Pour into molds and refrigerate for at least 4 hours until set.

Rice Pudding

Ingredients:

- 1 cup rice (short-grain)
- 4 cups milk
- ½ cup sugar
- 1 teaspoon vanilla extract
- Ground cinnamon for garnish

Instructions:

1. **Cook rice**: In a pot, combine rice and milk. Cook over low heat, stirring frequently, until rice is tender and mixture thickens.
2. **Add sugar and vanilla**: Stir in sugar and vanilla extract, cooking for a few more minutes.
3. **Serve**: Spoon into bowls and sprinkle with ground cinnamon.

Fruit Salad

Ingredients:

- 2 cups mixed fresh fruit (such as berries, melons, and grapes)
- 1 tablespoon honey
- 1 tablespoon lemon juice
- Fresh mint for garnish

Instructions:

1. **Prepare fruit**: Cut fruit into bite-sized pieces and place in a bowl.
2. **Mix dressing**: In a small bowl, whisk together honey and lemon juice.
3. **Combine**: Drizzle the dressing over the fruit and toss gently.
4. **Serve**: Garnish with fresh mint before serving.

Tiramisu

Ingredients:

- 1 cup strong brewed coffee (cooled)
- 3 tablespoons coffee liqueur (optional)
- 3 large eggs (separated)
- ½ cup sugar
- 1 cup mascarpone cheese
- 1 cup heavy cream (whipped)
- 20 ladyfinger cookies
- Cocoa powder for dusting

Instructions:

1. **Mix coffee**: Combine coffee and coffee liqueur in a shallow dish.
2. **Beat egg yolks**: In a bowl, beat egg yolks with sugar until thick and creamy.
3. **Add mascarpone**: Fold in mascarpone cheese and whipped cream.
4. **Layer**: Dip ladyfingers briefly in coffee and layer them in a dish. Spread half of the mascarpone mixture over, then repeat layers.
5. **Chill**: Refrigerate for at least 4 hours, then dust with cocoa powder before serving.

Chocolate Covered Strawberries

Ingredients:

- 1 pound fresh strawberries
- 8 ounces dark chocolate (chopped)
- 1 tablespoon coconut oil (optional)

Instructions:

1. **Melt chocolate**: In a microwave or double boiler, melt chocolate with coconut oil until smooth.
2. **Dip strawberries**: Dip each strawberry into the melted chocolate, allowing excess to drip off.
3. **Set**: Place dipped strawberries on a parchment-lined tray and refrigerate until chocolate hardens.

Coconut Ladoo

Ingredients:

- 2 cups shredded coconut
- 1 cup condensed milk
- 1 teaspoon cardamom powder
- ¼ cup chopped nuts (optional)

Instructions:

1. **Combine ingredients**: In a pan, combine shredded coconut, condensed milk, and cardamom powder. Cook on low heat, stirring continuously until mixture thickens.
2. **Cool mixture**: Allow the mixture to cool slightly, then form into small balls.
3. **Roll in coconut**: Optionally, roll ladoos in extra shredded coconut before serving.

Key Lime Pie (No-Bake)

Ingredients:

- 1 ½ cups graham cracker crumbs
- ½ cup unsalted butter (melted)
- 1 cup key lime juice
- 1 cup sweetened condensed milk
- 1 cup heavy whipping cream (whipped)
- Lime zest for garnish

Instructions:

1. **Prepare crust**: Mix graham cracker crumbs with melted butter and press into the bottom of a pie dish.
2. **Make filling**: In a bowl, combine key lime juice and sweetened condensed milk. Stir until well blended.
3. **Fold in cream**: Gently fold in the whipped cream until smooth.
4. **Chill**: Pour the filling into the crust and refrigerate for at least 4 hours or until set. Garnish with lime zest before serving.

Parfaits

Ingredients:

- 2 cups yogurt (flavored or plain)
- 2 cups granola
- 2 cups mixed berries (strawberries, blueberries, raspberries)
- Honey or maple syrup (optional)

Instructions:

1. **Layer ingredients**: In glasses or bowls, layer yogurt, granola, and mixed berries.
2. **Repeat layers**: Repeat layers until glasses are filled.
3. **Drizzle**: Optionally, drizzle honey or maple syrup on top before serving.

Strawberry Shortcake (No-Bake)

Ingredients:

- 2 cups strawberries (sliced)
- 1 cup heavy cream (whipped)
- 1 package store-bought pound cake (sliced)
- 2 tablespoons sugar (for strawberries)
- Mint for garnish (optional)

Instructions:

1. **Prepare strawberries**: Toss sliced strawberries with sugar and let sit for about 10 minutes.
2. **Assemble**: In serving dishes, layer slices of pound cake, whipped cream, and macerated strawberries.
3. **Serve**: Garnish with mint before serving.

Ice Cream Sundae

Ingredients:

- 4 cups vanilla ice cream
- ½ cup chocolate sauce
- ½ cup caramel sauce
- Chopped nuts (optional)
- Whipped cream
- Maraschino cherries for topping

Instructions:

1. **Scoop ice cream**: Place scoops of vanilla ice cream in bowls.
2. **Add toppings**: Drizzle with chocolate and caramel sauce, and sprinkle with chopped nuts if desired.
3. **Finish**: Top with whipped cream and a maraschino cherry before serving.

Cookie Dough Truffles

Ingredients:

- 1 cup all-purpose flour (heat-treated)
- ½ cup unsalted butter (softened)
- ½ cup brown sugar
- ¼ cup granulated sugar
- 1 teaspoon vanilla extract
- ½ cup mini chocolate chips
- 8 ounces chocolate (for coating)

Instructions:

1. **Mix dough**: In a bowl, cream together butter, brown sugar, and granulated sugar. Stir in flour, vanilla, and chocolate chips.
2. **Form balls**: Roll dough into small balls and place on a baking sheet. Freeze for about 30 minutes.
3. **Coat in chocolate**: Melt chocolate, dip each ball in chocolate, and return to the baking sheet to set.

Chia Seed Pudding

Ingredients:

- ½ cup chia seeds
- 2 cups almond milk (or any milk)
- 2 tablespoons honey or maple syrup
- 1 teaspoon vanilla extract
- Fresh fruit for topping

Instructions:

1. **Mix ingredients**: In a bowl, whisk together chia seeds, almond milk, honey, and vanilla until combined.
2. **Chill**: Refrigerate for at least 4 hours or overnight, stirring occasionally until thickened.
3. **Serve**: Top with fresh fruit before serving.

Pudding Cups

Ingredients:

- 2 cups milk
- ½ cup sugar
- ¼ cup cornstarch
- ¼ teaspoon salt
- 1 teaspoon vanilla extract

Instructions:

1. **Combine ingredients**: In a saucepan, whisk together sugar, cornstarch, and salt. Gradually add milk and cook over medium heat, stirring constantly until thickened.
2. **Add vanilla**: Remove from heat and stir in vanilla extract.
3. **Cool and serve**: Pour into cups and chill before serving.

Energy Bites

Ingredients:

- 1 cup oats
- ½ cup peanut butter
- ¼ cup honey
- ½ cup chocolate chips
- ¼ cup ground flaxseed

Instructions:

1. **Combine ingredients**: In a bowl, mix oats, peanut butter, honey, chocolate chips, and ground flaxseed until well combined.
2. **Form balls**: Roll the mixture into small balls and place on a baking sheet.
3. **Chill**: Refrigerate for about 30 minutes before serving.

Mocha Chocolate Truffles

Ingredients:

- 8 ounces dark chocolate (chopped)
- ½ cup heavy cream
- 1 tablespoon instant coffee granules
- Cocoa powder or chopped nuts for coating

Instructions:

1. **Heat cream**: In a saucepan, heat heavy cream until just simmering.
2. **Add chocolate**: Remove from heat, add chopped chocolate and coffee granules. Stir until smooth.
3. **Chill**: Refrigerate the mixture for about 2 hours until firm.
4. **Form truffles**: Scoop out small amounts and roll into balls.
5. **Coat**: Roll in cocoa powder or chopped nuts before serving.

Fruit Tart (No-Bake)

Ingredients:

- 1 ½ cups graham cracker crumbs
- ½ cup unsalted butter (melted)
- 1 cup cream cheese (softened)
- ½ cup powdered sugar
- 1 teaspoon vanilla extract
- 2 cups mixed fresh fruit

Instructions:

1. **Prepare crust**: Mix graham cracker crumbs with melted butter and press into the bottom of a tart pan.
2. **Make filling**: In a bowl, beat cream cheese, powdered sugar, and vanilla until smooth.
3. **Assemble**: Spread the cream cheese mixture over the crust and top with fresh fruit.
4. **Chill**: Refrigerate for at least 1 hour before serving.

Banana Pudding

Ingredients:

- 1 box vanilla pudding mix
- 2 cups milk
- 1 teaspoon vanilla extract
- 3 ripe bananas (sliced)
- 1 box vanilla wafers
- Whipped cream for topping

Instructions:

1. **Prepare pudding**: In a bowl, whisk together pudding mix, milk, and vanilla until thickened.
2. **Layer**: In a dish, layer vanilla wafers, banana slices, and pudding mixture.
3. **Repeat layers**: Repeat until ingredients are used up, finishing with pudding on top.
4. **Top**: Chill for at least 2 hours and top with whipped cream before serving.

Lemon Bars (No-Bake)

Ingredients:

- 1 ½ cups graham cracker crumbs
- ½ cup unsalted butter (melted)
- 1 cup sweetened condensed milk
- ½ cup lemon juice
- Zest of 1 lemon

Instructions:

1. **Prepare crust**: Mix graham cracker crumbs with melted butter and press into a baking dish.
2. **Make filling**: In a bowl, combine sweetened condensed milk, lemon juice, and lemon zest.
3. **Pour and chill**: Pour the filling over the crust and refrigerate for at least 3 hours until set.

S'mores Dip

Ingredients:

- 1 cup chocolate chips
- 1 cup mini marshmallows
- Graham crackers for dipping

Instructions:

1. **Layer ingredients**: In a baking dish, layer chocolate chips and top with mini marshmallows.
2. **Broil**: Place under the broiler for 2-3 minutes until marshmallows are golden.
3. **Serve**: Serve warm with graham crackers for dipping.

Chocolate Bark

Ingredients:

- 12 ounces dark chocolate (chopped)
- 1 cup mixed nuts or dried fruit (optional)

Instructions:

1. **Melt chocolate**: Melt chocolate in a microwave or double boiler until smooth.
2. **Spread**: Pour onto a parchment-lined baking sheet and spread evenly.
3. **Top**: Sprinkle with nuts or dried fruit if desired.
4. **Chill**: Refrigerate until set, then break into pieces.

Peanut Butter Balls

Ingredients:

- 1 cup peanut butter
- 1 cup powdered sugar
- 2 cups rice cereal
- 1 cup chocolate chips (for coating)

Instructions:

1. **Mix ingredients**: In a bowl, combine peanut butter, powdered sugar, and rice cereal until well mixed.
2. **Form balls**: Roll mixture into small balls and place on a baking sheet.
3. **Coat**: Melt chocolate chips and dip each ball in chocolate, then return to the baking sheet to set.

No-Bake Oatmeal Cookies

Ingredients:

- 1 cup rolled oats
- ½ cup peanut butter
- ½ cup honey
- ¼ cup cocoa powder
- ½ teaspoon vanilla extract

Instructions:

1. **Mix ingredients**: In a bowl, combine oats, peanut butter, honey, cocoa powder, and vanilla until well blended.
2. **Scoop**: Drop spoonfuls onto a baking sheet lined with parchment paper.
3. **Chill**: Refrigerate for at least 30 minutes before serving.

Marshmallow Fluff Dip

Ingredients:

- 1 cup marshmallow fluff
- 1 cup cream cheese (softened)
- 1 teaspoon vanilla extract
- Fresh fruit or graham crackers for dipping

Instructions:

1. **Mix ingredients**: In a bowl, beat together marshmallow fluff, cream cheese, and vanilla until smooth.
2. **Serve**: Transfer to a serving bowl and serve with fresh fruit or graham crackers for dipping.

Avocado Chocolate Mousse

Ingredients:

- 2 ripe avocados
- ½ cup cocoa powder
- ½ cup honey or maple syrup
- 1 teaspoon vanilla extract
- Pinch of salt

Instructions:

1. **Blend**: In a blender, combine avocados, cocoa powder, honey, vanilla, and salt until smooth and creamy.
2. **Chill**: Refrigerate for about 30 minutes before serving.

Frozen Yogurt Bark

Ingredients:

- 2 cups Greek yogurt
- 2 tablespoons honey
- ½ cup mixed berries (fresh or frozen)
- Optional toppings (nuts, granola, chocolate chips)

Instructions:

1. **Mix yogurt and honey**: In a bowl, mix Greek yogurt and honey until well combined.
2. **Spread**: Spread the yogurt mixture evenly on a parchment-lined baking sheet.
3. **Top**: Sprinkle with mixed berries and any additional toppings.
4. **Freeze**: Freeze for about 3-4 hours, then break into pieces.

Gelato

Ingredients:

- 2 cups whole milk
- 1 cup heavy cream
- ¾ cup sugar
- 1 teaspoon vanilla extract
- Optional flavorings (like fruit purees or chocolate)

Instructions:

1. **Heat ingredients**: In a saucepan, heat milk and cream until warm.
2. **Dissolve sugar**: Stir in sugar until dissolved. Remove from heat and add vanilla.
3. **Chill mixture**: Let cool and then refrigerate for at least 2 hours.
4. **Churn**: Pour into an ice cream maker and churn according to manufacturer instructions.

Frozen Banana Bites

Ingredients:

- 2 ripe bananas
- 1 cup chocolate chips
- 1 tablespoon coconut oil

Instructions:

1. **Slice bananas**: Cut bananas into bite-sized pieces and place on a parchment-lined baking sheet.
2. **Melt chocolate**: In a microwave-safe bowl, melt chocolate chips and coconut oil together.
3. **Dip bananas**: Dip each banana piece in the melted chocolate and return to the baking sheet.
4. **Freeze**: Freeze for about 1 hour until firm.

Meringue Cookies

Ingredients:

- 4 egg whites
- 1 cup sugar
- 1 teaspoon vanilla extract
- Pinch of salt

Instructions:

1. **Preheat oven**: Preheat the oven to 225°F (110°C).
2. **Beat egg whites**: In a clean bowl, beat egg whites and salt until soft peaks form.
3. **Add sugar**: Gradually add sugar while continuing to beat until stiff peaks form.
4. **Pipe onto baking sheet**: Spoon or pipe meringue onto a parchment-lined baking sheet.
5. **Bake**: Bake for 1.5 hours or until crisp.

Smoothie Bowl

Ingredients:

- 1 cup frozen fruit (banana, berries, etc.)
- ½ cup Greek yogurt
- ½ cup milk (or almond milk)
- Toppings (granola, seeds, fresh fruit)

Instructions:

1. **Blend ingredients**: In a blender, combine frozen fruit, yogurt, and milk until smooth.
2. **Pour and top**: Pour into a bowl and add your favorite toppings.

Frozen Cheesecake Bites

Ingredients:

- 8 ounces cream cheese (softened)
- ½ cup powdered sugar
- 1 teaspoon vanilla extract
- Graham cracker crumbs for coating

Instructions:

1. **Mix filling**: In a bowl, beat cream cheese, powdered sugar, and vanilla until smooth.
2. **Form bites**: Scoop small amounts and roll into balls.
3. **Coat**: Roll each ball in graham cracker crumbs.
4. **Freeze**: Place on a baking sheet and freeze until firm.

Sweet Potato Pie (No-Bake)

Ingredients:

- 1 ½ cups cooked and mashed sweet potatoes
- ½ cup sugar or sweetener of choice
- 1 teaspoon vanilla extract
- 1 teaspoon cinnamon
- 1 teaspoon nutmeg
- 1 cup whipped cream
- 1 pre-made graham cracker crust

Instructions:

1. **Mix ingredients**: In a bowl, combine mashed sweet potatoes, sugar, vanilla, cinnamon, and nutmeg until smooth.
2. **Fold in whipped cream**: Gently fold in whipped cream until well combined.
3. **Fill crust**: Pour the mixture into the graham cracker crust and smooth the top.
4. **Chill**: Refrigerate for at least 4 hours or until set before serving.

Nutella Mousse

Ingredients:

- 1 cup heavy cream
- ½ cup Nutella
- 1 teaspoon vanilla extract

Instructions:

1. **Whip cream**: In a bowl, whip heavy cream until soft peaks form.
2. **Fold in Nutella**: Gently fold in Nutella and vanilla until smooth and combined.
3. **Chill**: Spoon into serving dishes and refrigerate for 1-2 hours before serving.

Agar Jelly

Ingredients:

- 2 cups fruit juice (like mango or grape)
- 2 teaspoons agar-agar powder
- Sweetener to taste

Instructions:

1. **Mix agar with juice**: In a saucepan, combine agar-agar powder and fruit juice.
2. **Heat**: Bring to a boil, stirring continuously until agar is fully dissolved.
3. **Set in molds**: Pour the mixture into molds and let cool until set in the refrigerator.

Sweetened Condensed Milk Pudding

Ingredients:

- 1 can (14 ounces) sweetened condensed milk
- 2 cups milk
- 3 tablespoons cornstarch
- 1 teaspoon vanilla extract

Instructions:

1. **Mix ingredients**: In a saucepan, whisk together sweetened condensed milk, milk, cornstarch, and vanilla.
2. **Cook**: Heat over medium heat, stirring until thickened.
3. **Chill**: Pour into serving cups and refrigerate until set.

Fruit and Yogurt Cups

Ingredients:

- 2 cups yogurt (any flavor)
- 2 cups mixed fresh fruit (berries, banana, etc.)
- Granola for topping

Instructions:

1. **Layer ingredients**: In cups or bowls, layer yogurt, mixed fruit, and granola.
2. **Serve**: Repeat layers until cups are filled and serve immediately.

Rice Crispy Treats

Ingredients:

- 3 tablespoons butter
- 1 package (10 ounces) marshmallows
- 6 cups rice crispy cereal

Instructions:

1. **Melt butter**: In a saucepan, melt butter over low heat.
2. **Add marshmallows**: Stir in marshmallows until melted and smooth.
3. **Mix in cereal**: Remove from heat and mix in rice crispy cereal until well coated.
4. **Press into pan**: Press the mixture into a greased pan and let cool before cutting into squares.

No-Bake Granola Bars

Ingredients:

- 2 cups oats
- ½ cup nut butter (peanut or almond)
- ½ cup honey or maple syrup
- 1 cup mix-ins (nuts, dried fruit, chocolate chips)

Instructions:

1. **Mix ingredients**: In a bowl, combine oats, nut butter, honey, and mix-ins until well combined.
2. **Press into pan**: Press the mixture into a lined baking dish and refrigerate for at least 1 hour.
3. **Cut into bars**: Once set, cut into bars and serve.

Chocolate Avocado Pudding

Ingredients:

- 2 ripe avocados
- ½ cup cocoa powder
- ½ cup honey or maple syrup
- 1 teaspoon vanilla extract
- Pinch of salt

Instructions:

1. **Blend ingredients**: In a blender, combine avocados, cocoa powder, honey, vanilla, and salt until smooth and creamy.
2. **Chill**: Refrigerate for about 30 minutes before serving.

Orange Panna Cotta

Ingredients:

- 1 ½ cups heavy cream
- ½ cup sugar
- 1 teaspoon vanilla extract
- Zest of 1 orange
- 1 packet (2 ½ teaspoons) gelatin
- 2 tablespoons cold water
- ½ cup fresh orange juice

Instructions:

1. **Dissolve gelatin**: In a small bowl, sprinkle gelatin over cold water and let it sit for 5 minutes.
2. **Heat cream**: In a saucepan, combine heavy cream, sugar, vanilla, and orange zest. Heat until sugar is dissolved but do not boil.
3. **Combine**: Remove from heat, add the gelatin mixture and orange juice, and stir until dissolved.
4. **Chill**: Pour into serving cups and refrigerate for at least 4 hours until set.

Lemon Coconut Energy Bites

Ingredients:

- 1 cup rolled oats
- ½ cup shredded coconut
- ½ cup almond butter
- ¼ cup honey or maple syrup
- Zest of 1 lemon
- 1 tablespoon lemon juice

Instructions:

1. **Mix ingredients**: In a bowl, combine all ingredients and mix until well combined.
2. **Form balls**: Roll mixture into small balls and place on a baking sheet.
3. **Chill**: Refrigerate for 30 minutes to firm up before serving.

No-Bake Pumpkin Pie

Ingredients:

- 1 ½ cups pumpkin puree
- ½ cup sugar or sweetener of choice
- 1 teaspoon vanilla extract
- 1 teaspoon pumpkin pie spice
- 1 ½ cups whipped cream
- 1 pre-made graham cracker crust

Instructions:

1. **Mix filling**: In a bowl, combine pumpkin puree, sugar, vanilla, and pumpkin pie spice until smooth.
2. **Fold in whipped cream**: Gently fold in whipped cream until fully incorporated.
3. **Fill crust**: Pour the filling into the graham cracker crust and smooth the top.
4. **Chill**: Refrigerate for at least 4 hours before serving.

Berry Crumble (Stovetop)

Ingredients:

- 2 cups mixed berries (fresh or frozen)
- 2 tablespoons sugar
- 1 tablespoon cornstarch
- 1 tablespoon lemon juice
- 1 cup oats
- ¼ cup flour
- ¼ cup brown sugar
- ½ teaspoon cinnamon
- ¼ cup butter, melted

Instructions:

1. **Prepare berry mixture**: In a skillet, combine berries, sugar, cornstarch, and lemon juice. Cook over medium heat until bubbly and thickened.
2. **Mix crumble**: In a bowl, combine oats, flour, brown sugar, cinnamon, and melted butter until crumbly.
3. **Combine and cook**: Sprinkle the crumble over the berry mixture in the skillet and cover. Cook on low for 10-15 minutes until the topping is golden and crisp.

Chocolate Chip Cookie Ice Cream Sandwiches

Ingredients:

- 1 batch of chocolate chip cookie dough (store-bought or homemade)
- 2 cups ice cream (any flavor)

Instructions:

1. **Bake cookies**: Preheat oven and bake cookies according to dough instructions. Let cool completely.
2. **Assemble sandwiches**: Place a scoop of ice cream between two cookies and press gently to form a sandwich.
3. **Freeze**: Place sandwiches in the freezer for about 30 minutes to set before serving.

Peanut Butter Fudge

Ingredients:

- 1 cup peanut butter
- 1 cup powdered sugar
- ½ cup butter, softened
- 1 teaspoon vanilla extract

Instructions:

1. **Mix ingredients**: In a bowl, combine peanut butter, powdered sugar, butter, and vanilla until smooth.
2. **Pour into pan**: Spread the mixture into a greased baking dish.
3. **Chill**: Refrigerate for at least 2 hours until firm, then cut into squares.

Tofu Chocolate Pudding

Ingredients:

- 1 block (14 ounces) silken tofu, drained
- ½ cup cocoa powder
- ½ cup maple syrup or honey
- 1 teaspoon vanilla extract

Instructions:

1. **Blend ingredients**: In a blender, combine tofu, cocoa powder, maple syrup, and vanilla until smooth and creamy.
2. **Chill**: Spoon into serving dishes and refrigerate for at least 30 minutes before serving.

Raw Vegan Brownies

Ingredients:

- 1 cup walnuts
- 1 cup dates, pitted
- ½ cup cocoa powder
- ½ teaspoon vanilla extract
- Pinch of salt

Instructions:

1. **Process ingredients**: In a food processor, combine walnuts, dates, cocoa powder, vanilla, and salt until a sticky dough forms.
2. **Press into pan**: Press the mixture into a lined baking dish.
3. **Chill**: Refrigerate for at least 1 hour before cutting into squares and serving.

Chocolate Coconut Truffles

Ingredients:

- 1 cup dark chocolate chips
- ½ cup full-fat coconut milk
- 1 cup shredded coconut
- 2 tablespoons maple syrup (optional)
- Pinch of salt

Instructions:

1. **Melt chocolate**: In a saucepan, heat chocolate chips and coconut milk over low heat until melted and smooth.
2. **Mix ingredients**: Stir in shredded coconut, maple syrup (if using), and salt until well combined.
3. **Chill mixture**: Refrigerate for about 30 minutes until firm.
4. **Form truffles**: Scoop out small portions and roll them into balls.
5. **Coat and chill**: Roll truffles in additional shredded coconut, place on a baking sheet, and refrigerate until set.

Fruit Popsicles

Ingredients:

- 2 cups fresh or frozen fruit (e.g., berries, mango, or banana)
- 1 cup juice (e.g., orange juice, coconut water) or yogurt
- 2 tablespoons honey or maple syrup (optional)

Instructions:

1. **Blend ingredients**: In a blender, combine fruit, juice or yogurt, and sweetener (if using). Blend until smooth.
2. **Pour mixture**: Pour the mixture into popsicle molds, leaving a little space at the top for expansion.
3. **Insert sticks**: Insert popsicle sticks and freeze for at least 4 hours, or until solid.
4. **Unmold and serve**: To remove, run warm water over the outside of the molds for a few seconds, then gently pull out the popsicles.

www.ingramcontent.com/pod-product-compliance
Lightning Source LLC
LaVergne TN
LVHW081336060526
838201LV00055B/2674